Leaning
Into It

Leaning Into It

Poems

RIK EMMETT

Published by ECW Press
665 Gerrard Street East
Toronto, Ontario, Canada M4M 1Y2
416-694-3348 / info@ecwpress.com

MISFIT

Editor for the Press: Michael Holmes / a misFit Book
Copyeditor: Emily Schultz
Cover design: Jess Albert
Illustrations: Rik Emmett
Author photo: John Blacker

LIBRARY AND ARCHIVES CANADA CATALOGUING IN PUBLICATION

Title: Leaning into it : poems / Rik Emmett.

Names: Emmett, Rik, author.

Identifiers: Canadiana (print) 20250320347 | Canadiana (ebook) 20250320363

ISBN 978-1-77041-828-8 (softcover)
ISBN 978-1-77852-537-7 (ePub)
ISBN 978-1-77852-538-4 (PDF)

Subjects: LCGFT: Poetry.

Classification: LCC PS8609.M64 L43 2026 | DDC C811/.6—dc23

This book is funded in part by the Government of Canada. *Ce livre est financé en partie par le gouvernement du Canada.* We acknowledge the support of the Canada Council for the Arts. *Nous remercions le Conseil des arts du Canada de son soutien.* We would like to acknowledge the funding support of the Ontario Arts Council (OAC) and the Government of Ontario for their support. We also acknowledge the support of the Government of Ontario through the Ontario Book Publishing Tax Credit, and through Ontario Creates.

Canada

Canada Council for the Arts | Conseil des arts du Canada

Ontario

ONTARIO ARTS COUNCIL
CONSEIL DES ARTS DE L'ONTARIO
an Ontario government agency
un organisme du gouvernement de l'Ontario

ONTARIO CREATES

PRINTED AND BOUND IN CANADA

PRINTING: COACH HOUSE 5 4 3 2 1

To my family
and to the family of misfits everywhere
who keep leaning into a good fight for virtue
using poetry and music
believing in its imperatives
in the war against ugly powermongers
who fight dirty

Contents

PART 1
The Book of Alvaro Follis

PART 2
Venting

PART 3

Outside In—Coming to Terms

PART 4

Inside Out—Exercising, Exorcising

PART 5

Beyond Me

PART 1

The Book of Alvaro Follis

Alvaro Follis

Alvaro—as in guardian / observer / watchman
Follis, as in a foolish, bellowing, bag of wind
fanning the flames of a fire
to burn away hypocrisy / ego / vanity

In the grand traditions of ancient Rome's balatrones
and England's Robert Armin & Thomas Killigrew
Alvie speaks truth to power

court jester / minstrel troubadour / fool
graffiti scribbler—the deck's wild card
dealt as Shakespearean comic relief

mostly he just talks to his marotte
which, curiously, currently resembles a Neumann U 87

why? you may ask: why not? he might respond

if it please the court: it goes to motive

it all goes to *motive*

First Person

The modern conservative is engaged in one of man's oldest exercises in moral philosophy; that is, the search for a superior moral justification for selfishness.
—JOHN KENNETH GALBRAITH

capital *I*
skinniest, plainest letter in the alphabet
biggest troublemaker
no depth perspective
no dimension
no shapes, no curves
I-yi-*yi*-yi-*yi*

try to get it out of your system, scribe

me
arpeggiate that up & down
(like a diva, warming up on a favourite subject)

me
me *me*
me *me*
me *me*

try your best to expunge the first person, correspondent
minstrel jongleur troubadour

banish it from the page, distiller
don't let it cloud the perception
walk around the sculpture in progress
in other shoes, with other eyes

there's no problem with righteousness
it's self-righteous selfishness that becomes a toxic problem

seek the objectivity of otherness

Four Wishes—A Toast (Or a Prayer)
Offered by Alvaro Follis

when the sun comes up tomorrow
may it guide each step you take
may your joy outweigh your sorrow
in the world that you create
may your lucky stars align on down
whatever road you choose
with lovelight shining all around
to chase away the blues

Show Business

the fool lays down his marotte
the troubadour puts aside his guitarra
yet these tools of the trade still provoke the jester
the tickling seduction of the avocation, the whispers
from Calliope Erato Euterpe Polyhymnia Terpsichore and Thalia

why me? he asks
and they respond from the other side of the mirror
why do you still feel the need to ask? why so worked up?

he was mostly trying to work things out, for his own edification
could any revelation be of value to others?
might they find what makes him tick   & ticks him off   entertaining?

the marotte says   *you know why you did it*
you fell in love with the danger of making a spectacle of yourself
the *show* was a life of show *biz*
and the show must go on in this *business* of show
and the showdown will always be, to show up and show off

he felt he must offer his confession—yet the marotte reminded him
if they smelled your fear in the stalls, they could eat you alive
or simply leave you for dead, as your own fear consumed you anyway
precious little business to be had in a show of weakness
careers, after all, are built on shows of strength

the muses whisper—*you love chasing us*
even though, after a while, you knew full well we could never be caught
but the thrill is in the chase
and you're addicted to the avocation, based upon our invitations
so go ahead and write us a poem: offer us a prayer
sing us your answers to your questions
show us, troubadour
show us

The Last Refuge of Scoundrels

let us speak of curious things
podcasters, poets, philosopher kings

after Wallace Stevens & Zimmerman
these Crispins & jokers & thieves
jongleurs & troubadours—court jesters all
work up the crowd at the masquerade ball

reduced to the run of instincts—distilled to that essence
the latest vanguard summon the will to skirmish
but lack the power / vision / strength to change the world
or modify human nature

it's hard enough to change yourself
still—you've got to admire a good set of changes

so now—let us speak of trivial things
the posting of poets, philosopher kings
twittering tiktokers, x'ing in silos
following ghosts who whisper in shadows

the bars of entry have been lowered
and the digital tsunami redefines the playing field
moves the goalposts—eviscerates the rule book

presumably the decline of civilization will continue
continue to fall
fall apart

so now—let us speak of a meaningless thing
a senior citizen philosopher king
playing the fool to the bitter end
phrasing the lines in his games of pretend

and while it's been said
that *the last refuge of a scoundrel is a cloak of false patriotism*
in the temper of these times almost everything rings false
because—who gets to define "last refuge"?
and how to identify scoundrels? since, by definition
they *defy definitions*

Coming Clean

poet? what in the name of all that's sacred
goes to motivation?

it's partly the search for clues in the abstract
the surrealism & impressionism of life
the discovery of truth as a perspective
a point of view

there's also the integrity of the architecture
fascination with the chemistry

he can only guess at what shaped him into a court jester
and that guessing game is surely a big part of it
not just the cryptic crossword pleasure
but the motivation of the game developer

there's frustration at the universal chaos
filtering on down to the masquerade
disguising the failures of law & order
peace & good government

there's heartache in the wreckage—the ruins of civilization
the damage that hasn't quite killed (*not yet, anyway*)

so the gig lies in securing the survivor testimony
witness & victim statements—evidence for the prosecution:
getting it on the public record and offered up as prayers to the cosmos

the court jester knows too well, he must remain a moving target
do or say nothing that pins him down
float like a butterfly, put on a show
leave 'em laughing when you go

once again, good people, and if it please the court
the evidence in itself is self-evident
the telltale exhibits
                    of an exhibitionist

The Hunger for More

there are so many other things that go to motivation
words that drift on the wind, phrases that sing of the earth and sky
the sweep of clouds—the scattering rustling of leaves

language to translate the ineffable
akin to the red hand on the Maltravieso cave walls
the pig-hunting Sulawesi

your humble correspondent stood on a wall
of the Wupatki ruins in Arizona, gazing west
hearing the centuries whispering in the rhythms of his blood

there's a kind of reasoning towards belief
incremental, tiny leaps of faith, in *thought word & deed*
that addictive feeling, that the work has its own gravity
writing itself

it's the blatant challenge of an empty page
and an itchy pen
the ambition of a commoner, to gain entrance to the royal court
(and the court of public opinion)
there, to play the fool

it's dreams that dance among the stars
contemplation and prayer

blood that remembers spring
even as winter approaches

ah yes—the prospect of eternal oblivion, after all of this glorious ego
so—all of this scratching and noodling are preludes to forever
when "is" becomes "was"
. . . there's all of that—and more

the hunger for *more*

Avocation

beneath & beyond the celebration of the body electric
the singing athletic glorification of youth
there resides a need to go deeper
a distillation of process, to find the courage
articulate the private, go on the record for posterity
to acknowledge & satisfy the nature of synapses
collisions of head, heart & soul

to describe how light plays in reflection & shadow
how words dance & weave amongst threads in the tapestry

armchair workouts, rewarding intellectual integration
of hemispheres, neurons firing along degrading pathways
stitching together the worn & frayed

affirmative action that hooks up connections
that feel inevitable / undeniable / elemental

avocation, calling at its most fundamental

can you hear that?

the stardust is talking

Reflections On & Off Stardust

how much of one's life gets spent in distraction?
waiting longing wishing hoping—sleeping
doing one thing while dreaming about something else?
how much of one's time gets squandered, polluted, wasted
chasing after something that comes to nothing?
pushing when it was smarter to pull—
pulling when wiser to push?

minutes hours days weeks years
when one's senses have gone numb
when one could have been seeing hearing smelling touching tasting feeling
indulging in somesthesia

and in the end, what does it amount to?
even the somethings that managed to actually *come to something*
all that waiting longing sleeping dreaming
all that squandering & chasing
all that sensationalizing

will the sum be greater than the parts
when one fades from grey to white to black
beyond the relentless currents of gravity
where one's hydrogen & oxygen return to big bang vapour
and the rest—the carbon—is detritus: debris:
        stardust
drifting in the hurly burly of those still navigating their push & pull?

one longs and dreams that their particulate might still capture some light
reflect & sparkle so that creatures with the gift of flight
        flights of fancy
will feel compelled to gather some up
and use it
                to feather their nests

Choosing Stardust

choices, options: dozens—hundreds, every day
times billions of people on the planet
conscious, unconscious
initiated by us, and visited upon us by others

meanwhile—what's happening
in an infinite stretch of imaginative multiverses
where different choices were made?
every choice opening up yet another infinite stretch
of the infinite multiverse

one day
(for the billions upon billions of imaginative picky choosers on this planet)
an asteroid might strike: or the sun could emit a deadly flare
or the Vogons of Douglas Adams could arrive
to clear out this solar system for their intergalactic hyperspace freeway

then it won't matter if you wore the patterned socks or the stripes
or went with the salad instead of the fries
or if you waited for happy hour, or if you prayed five times a day

so by all means—choose what you will
choose frivolously, choose wisely
choose your sacrament—choose your poison

this court jester chooses to believe
there's only one universe that matters
and our rituals provide for our mortal creature comforts
until, one day, inevitably
we shall all return to the solitary universe
of stardust

The Wake

oh, I can tell you what Alvie was good at.
he was good at doing selfish things, and sharing that with strangers.
his family? his loved ones?
they'd grown numb and bored of his parlour tricks.

Alvaro had no instincts for domestic commitment.
no natural inclination towards cooking, housekeeping
for things like Christmas shopping or gift wrapping.
for that kind of stuff, he was mediocre
heading towards downright lousy.

at least he could be a source of amusement for those around him—
mocked for his shortcomings.
they salvaged tidbits of revenge by serving out guilt
over the responsibilities and burdens he defaulted on:
half-smirking about his half-hearted, half-assed failures at the domestic.

he was a whole lotta jazz hands to the public
but kinda half-baked, half-measure, outta the spotlight.

that's the truth.
and Alvie loved the truth
he was pretty good at trying to speak the truth
and I'm pretty sure he'd agree with what I'm telling you.

PART 2

Venting

Fixations

who wants to play a game you can't win?

i'd vote for a Bertrand Russell or a George Carlin
but dudes like that never run, and who can blame 'em?
they'd be unelectable

politicians have to pretend to cater to the status quo—
unenlightened, irrational, dark age fixations

we can't begin to repair the broken systems
the rules of the games
the nature of these beasts

the likely suspects—the *candidates*—
know the rules of the game: know the fix we're in
cuz the fix is in, and they want in on it

the biggest fixation of them all
is the power & the glory, forever & ever
amen

and that's a game that court jesters can never win
they're not even in the contest

if they're lucky, they just might get to be
                                                the halftime entertainment

They Launch Armadas

Whoever undertakes to set himself up as a judge of Truth and Knowledge is shipwrecked by the laughter of the gods.
—EDMUND BURKE, "PREFACE TO BRISSOT'S ADDRESS TO HIS CONSTITUENTS"

singular can now be *they*

they wrote a poem
they are launching their armada

with subjective first person expunged from the dialogue
it is from the lofty heights of a more perfect perception
that they may pursue the ideals of objective omniscience
optimistic utopians, unencumbered by fallibility
free
to make new suggestions for new arrangements
organize to accumulate power, then
make demands: impose expectations: manifest entitlement
dismantle privilege and hierarchies of meritocracy
under flags of freedom & equality

ah, power
they're working out the exercise of authority—
the responsibility of their privilege

they are launching their armadas

yet—without the balance of an awareness of the absurd
and the humility of a sense of humour
we are deaf to the laughter of gods, new & old

behold the wreckage of armadas
crashing upon the rocky shoals
listen to the roaring of the wind

they are us

me & you

Rules of Engagement (Learn the Hard Way)

we learn the hard way
can't reason with unreasonable people or rationalize with the irrational
can't save some people from themselves
can't extend the benefit of the doubt to belligerent bullies, vigilantes, vandals—
those who don't respect the boundaries of others, as if there's no such thing as
those who cannot fend for themselves—children, the aged, or the sick

in a dog-eat-dog world of rugged individualism
it's every armed citizen for themselves
and their constitutional right to bear arms
their right to erase lines
cross 'em, move 'em, draw their own new ones
right on over into your backyard, your bedroom
inside your head, inside your womb
flout laws—rewrite 'em
rig the game to get power: flex it. keep it.
enact their own sense of common sense
cuz *that's what power does*

load the bench with bias
which only confirms the system's corrupt prejudices
the new rules of engagement are:
bend, break, change the game, the venue, the definitions of the universe
lie, cheat & deny
while calling everyone else a phony *fake news* mythomaniac—
ah, mythomaniacs! *nation-builders: tribal chiefs: representatives of their gods*
flag-wavers, with the conviction of destiny on their side

so what we keep teaching each other, without the slightest
acknowledgement
of our track record for hypocrisy
is that we're just gonna keep right on
learning the hard way

Cry Freedom

According to the Canadian Charter of Rights and Freedoms,
freedom is "subject only to such reasonable limits prescribed by law
as can be demonstrably justified in a free and democratic society."

freedom is not some undefined idealistic boundless dream
it's always a work in progress, subject to *reason* and *law*
except when it gets unreasonable and downright illegal, which is often

perhaps that's why "freedom fighters" do not feel democratically obliged
to convince the general public that self-righteous self-importance
isn't conjuring up their myopic blindness

various shades of misguided incoherence claim "freedom" as a licence
to fuck with peace, order and good government
as cross words lead to crossed swords
the pettiness of petty crime masquerading as legal protest
is still criminal

willful ignorance remains the all-time champion equal-opportunity employer

those smart enough to know they don't have very many answers
keep getting subjected to those who are convinced they *do* know
what's best for *everybody*
while they continually demonstrate
that they don't even know what's best for themselves
yet refuse to operate from a position of humility

democracy is being murdered
the cause of death
is ten thousand cuts of ignorance

Chaos Theory

mirror doesn't lie—brain interprets the vision
heart doesn't lie—head processes & interprets the sensation
    opinions
all the assholes in the funhouse of mirrors have got 'em
    including the court minstrel

a deluge of images and reflections comes pouring through the screens
    of justification & rationalization & hypocrisy

oh, the hypocrisy

so The Word becomes carnate
through the brain or the body politic
and the evolutionary imperative asserts itself
through random genetic mutations, experiments, tangents
coping mechanisms within the chaos
and here we find ourselves

                standing in front of our mirrors

Justified Left & Right

Fear is the main source of superstition, and one of the main sources of cruelty.
To conquer fear is the beginning of wisdom.
—BERTRAND RUSSELL

The basket of deplorables . . . The racist, sexist,
homophobic, xenophobic, Islamaphobic—you name it.
And unfortunately there are people like that.
—HILLARY CLINTON

and so we must begin   again and again
as the digital technology strings run through the amplifying social noise
from angry protest to misplaced misguided misinformed indignation & selfishness

the politics of panic play out so far behind the curve
it's *always* too little too late
always running a deficit, before & after the fact
majorities held hostage by one minority or another after another after another

the rhetoric of fear makes for strange bedfellows
libertarians & anarchists, vigilantes & insurrectionists
an unholy alliance of evangelists, eco-warriors & white supremacists
the left shouts at the right and the right squalls back
neither extreme listens cuz
they're in love with the sound of their own voices
(you too, jester? well, at least it gives you pause—
at least the words on the page are *passive* aggression)
where does aggressive aggression get us? where does it leave us? except
deeper in the trenches
behind the wedges

cry freedom! for whom? from what?
there's never any freedom from the bullshit
of co-opting & sloganeering & flag-waving—
all irony lost on conspiracy theorists
as mythomaniacs are the biggest suckers for *fake news* in the first place
and *omg* do they ever hate hate *hate*
to get called out for being suckers

in this grand experiment of human ego—this custodial journey on planet Earth
the propaganda of opinion outranks & outflanks fact
for those who insist their own ideas of "nation" must come first
in the race for the lifeboats, as the mother ship is sinking

from a rickety platform of scattershot grievances
riddled with incoherent contradictions
a hodgepodge of protest theorists believe
their own frustration & anger deserves precedence
over the tired exasperation and disappointment of everyone else
as if the silent and law-abiding have not known the inconveniences
and tragedies of sickness, economic hardship and death

hey—Jacob Chansley had his self-righteous smug smiling libertarian moment
as he sat in the speaker's chair
an exercise of freedom that cost him his freedom
well—freedom comes at a cost to everyone
it's just that some don't accept the chafe of the outlay
with the same equanimity as others

pollsters say—solidify the base—preach to the choir
but no matter which side of the aisle
you claim, no matter which side of the bed
you were forced to get out of this morning
there's no end of the issue
in the truncheons and war measures of the riot squad
or the assault-rifle barrels of a vigilante militia

fashionable digital fascists
turn out to be a bunch of Caledon Nathan Hockleys
crying freedom & equality
aboard what they always assumed was their "unsinkable" mother ship
strong-arming their way onto the lifeboats

proverbial pride, abusing its way
ahead of the proverbial fall

Depths

There's a sucker born every minute.
—VARIOUS CON MEN & GAMBLERS OF THE MID-NINETEENTH CENTURY

No one in this world . . . has ever lost money by underestimating the intelligence of the great masses of the plain people.
—H. L. MENCKEN

Never underestimate the power of stupid people in large groups.
—GEORGE CARLIN

from an epidemic of conspiracy theories, one plot is indisputable—
the naked ambition of the egomaniacal, the autocratic, the tyrannical, the dictatorial
to take advantage of gullibility

across the full spectrum, there's so much superficial, shallow human activity
yet the depth & breadth of willful ignorance is astounding
so low down, so far out into the territory where principle gets confused with self-interest
which is a fallacy common to extremists of the ultra-far-right *and* left

how low can you go? how far out can you get?
because—*maybe there's a different dimension to depth*

depth can provide perspective, wisdom: perceive a spectrum
informed by sadness, disappointment, loss
therefore, it knows consideration: compassion: polite courtesy: social grace: diplomacy

so maybe it's more a question of how deep you care to dig
or where you choose to dig

because digging deep into shit
means you're still deep in shit

Work Ethic

how it used to work didn't work well for everyone
so that's not how it works,   anymore
of course—now nothing is working well, actually
except our strong, finishing kick in the race towards extinction

liberal democracy is a spent force
and a court jester will now offer details of how & why

the manifest destiny of rugged individualism
exhausts itself through the stripping & plundering of resources
its short-sighted futility
(exercising greed and calling it the freedom of constitutional rights)
is a cancer that cannibalizes the host

the demon desperation to fight like hell
to break the final straws of a social contract
and reject notions of compromise
is the destructive paradox of freedom

our blindness to the consequential realities of a digital universe
that shrunk the globe by fracturing it into multitudes of selfish parties—
well, *that ain't workin'*

so the party's over

the work ethic is now about splintered demographic tribal special interests:
petty provincial parochial sanctimonious self-righteous ecclesiastical dogmatic
jingo-xeno-wingnuts,   fighting over dwindling water holes

good luck with that, *kids*

Sloganeering (The Common-Sense Revolution)

Our major obligation is not to mistake slogans for solutions.
—EDWARD R. MURROW

aim your message at your base: base instincts fashion slogans for focus group polling
slicken up candidates to pivot & slip to their talking points
no good answer? change the question

ordinary citizens yearning for social order & good government
only get political leadership adept at betraying the pull of a moral compass
disillusioned by systems & bureaucrats, losing faith in humanity:
misanthropy growing, weary & defeated by unrelenting greed:
one could just spit at the posturing & pivoting & positioning of players
spreading the poison of toxic partnerships

cultural & social manipulations make gerrymandering bedfellows of the self-righteous
the fundamentalists, populists, libertarians, insurrectionists
headed on vision quests back into their wildernesses
meanwhile—far across the line, sharing that same strange bed
there's the left—crippled by its own perceptions of tyranny
obsessed with their aggrievements

no more middle class, no more middle ground
just a no-man's-land where climate change reduces the planet to wasteland
but by all means—
bump issues to committees for further study: schedule more dog & pony shows
debates that ring hollow, offering & settling nothing

the political supremacy of supernatural man-made gods shape this land
burning it out into a map of strategic voting blocks, parochial regionalism
wedge politics

the common-sense revolution was never an operational systematic platform—
it was just another slogan

more's the fucking pity

Bones to Pick

beyond pronouns, and the language of -*isms*
far beyond elder abuse
there are bleached white bones to pick

the history of ghosts gets rewritten
bronzed heads roll
the broad brushstrokes of blood-red war paint splatter memorials
as new Jacobins reconcile ancient thoughts & words & outdated deeds

without a trace of irony
in an illogical chronological class war
heads are judged, tried, convicted & decapitated
in the streets of the people's courts

truth is reconciled by the era's most honourable, as
the evil that men do lives after them
and the good is oft interred with their bones

start up the bandwagons

there are bones to pick

Mission Accomplished

bandwagons thunder round the issues
a riot mob ransacks The Capitol
as others stampede past burning churches
toppling statues, dancing & pissing on graves
trampling goodwill, brutalizing good faith
as if it never existed

somewhere in all the havoc
thin fine lines between reconciliation and revenge
get obliterated

there's no inclination towards consensus
to work together
to head the bandwagons off at the pass

the blunt points of mob mentality
are designed to strike with intimidation
to roll out fearsome wagons
to the clarion call of their air horns
the beat of their war drums
to disguise and conceal the hollow trampling
and obliteration of thin fine lines

rampages of outrage
inflame towards mayhem & anarchy
a dangerous world teeters into chaos

¡ mission accomplished !

Erosion

viruses make humanity fragile
humanity made the planet unstable

politics degraded the public trust

with the splintering disintegration
of our greedy defiant
protesting posturing
parochial provincial
far left and far right
it's all
          sliding
                    downhill

disappearing into the oceans
into the atmosphere

where there used to be good faith

now

          there's
                    only
                              erosion

Bother

why bother with boiling seething op-ed?

organizing the departments, the state matters
the ministries of foreign affairs, transportation & communication
human resources
reconciling the personal with the provincial & federal
the global & the universal

trying to come to terms with mortality

why bother?
why bother to build an orrery of the orbits?

because

because they cut right through
the intersection of the head and the heart

because lack of common sense
must be taken to task by reason, transparency, accountability

someone has to build a bigger picture
because in the give & take
the defence must raise objections
to those who are mostly on the take

so we must bother
    if only to set up
        some kind of defence
            against barbarians at the gate

                and to contain & restrain
                  the barbarian within

Has Been (We Pilgrims Pro*gress*)

behold the pilgrims, on their diverse pathways

the young, the bold who fortune favours
have spring in their step
raring for challenges
instigators gearing up, looking for a good fight
hunting, secure within their tribe

the old have become lame
vulnerable, battle-worn, tired
at best, philosophical—losing their religion
the ranks of survivors have thinned out
the campaigns ground 'em down, came at a cost
assuming some truths to be self-evident
makes them easy targets now
the tribe's front-line warriors
naturally select to leave 'em behind
as the young firebrands say
meh,
whatever it was
was what it *was*
but now this—*this* is what it is
and will be what it shall be
our truth can reconcile history

ardently they survey their quest, map out their campaign
basking in the illuminated revelations of fresh torchlight fire
exposing the weaknesses of old scars, wrinkles & fault lines
ancient dragons & monsters will be slain and spoils subdivided
according to the splintered, fragmented demographics
and wisdom of the newly anointed
doubling down on their thinking & speaking in their brave new world
filtering grievances
reinventing constitutional privilege
the currency & vitality of the entitled

some old pilgrims get vertigo from the déjà vu
because this is what power is, what it does
it has no time, no truck, no purchase, no real estate
for compassion—for has-beens

has been   *has been*
act your age & own your shame
you say your journey *has been* hard
has been treacherous
but your paths were false
has been   *has been*

digital age discernment
is far more discriminating than it ever was
damaged goods & discounted stories
must accept the bright & shining ambition
of judgment
rewriting history

behold the pilgrims
on diverse pathways
the young paving the way
towards the future
                    leaving roadkill behind

laughter echoes faintly from old paths that head down
into the valley of the shadows of what has been

the acolytes of new gods are making the most of their time
taking their turn
yet other turns will surely come

and somehow, this escapes the young
the bold who fortune favours

for what was, was
what has been, has been
what is, is
and what will be
shall be

Determination

new deals, new cards, in the games of us & them
new definitions: more clarifications / complications / specifications
the inclusion of these statistical issues of issue
are weighted in the new deals

money & power arise from real estate
accumulating accordingly
politics will be conducted & manipulated
cards will be played again & again
lines will be drawn & redrawn

oh, the new tide is rising
and some human sacrifices will have to be made
exorcisms must be performed
equalities / opportunities / freedoms
must be politically & legally reverse engineered
meritocracies will be re-evaluated and retrofitted
cooperation will be offered or sanctions will be imposed
inquisitions will lead to impositions as the new deals require—
they require this   *determination*

the dealers (and the casino owners) believe it counterproductive to stop
to ponder predetermined political realities:
the illogical premises and fundamentally flawed foundations

they prefer the momentum of profiteering progress

these entirely human affairs are subject to an imaginary
supernatural supremacy
overruled and governed by the metaphysical
all *determinations* subject to
                    this archaic *predetermination*

Old & New

a quorum of the new order
will oversee the imposition of the new deals
there will be new equalities—
will new bosses differ from the old?
what does it matter?
old architecture eventually
gets torn down for redevelopment
monuments & memorials get removed
in the name of progress
programs and systems get remade
become unrecognizable
                    meh—they sucked anyways
meritocracies will be dismantled
                    meh—they sucked too

the new merit shall have calculations of blood quantum
political & legal engineering

new eventually grows old
but for now
        now and then
                then again
        tomorrow and tomorrow and tomorrow
                                    accounts must be *reconciled*

Theatres of the Absurd

imagine—international networks of professional sports leagues
conducting billion-dollar businesses, daily, as usual
so that we can—as Seinfeld says—
cheer for laundry
in the gladiatorial bread & circus shows

meanwhile—every day—children die of malnutrition
and a lack of clean water
as floods & tornados & wild weather fluctuations
keep on comin'

imagine—climate change deniers and
anti-vaxxers, anti-maskers, anti-abortionists, anti-everythingers
so angry in their righteous indignation
chanting obscenities in front of their kids
and indulging in petty crimes of insurrection
civil disobedience as selfish myopia

then they go to church, cuz god is that golden rule of love
they take the kids for ice cream
cuz even a freedom protest convoy
can be an innocent family vacay

meanwhile—we set new statistical records for emergency departments
intensive care units: drug abuse: mental health care

imagine—so much rheum, spitting into the wind
warfare raging, in the comic darkness
as we cheer for our gladiators & mercenaries
and twirl our towels

helicopter that laundry! fire off them air horns!

nothing absurd about us folks

Venting Rage at the Outrageous World

pay no attention to that man behind the curtain

he's just venting rage
at the outrageous world

but he's harmless & powerless
old & grey
fading into irrelevance
just ignore him

all this whingeing
and whining
not banging
but whimpering

he may not be going quietly
but he's a goner
he just doesn't want to accept it yet

just ignore it
cancel it out
and it'll all be over

soon enough

PART 3

Outside In
Coming to Terms

Mind the Gap (Free Will)

in the seam of a concrete sidewalk
there's a windblown seed, waiting on a drop of rain
a tiny ray of sunlight

in the thin purple lines between courageous and foolhardy
between the polarities of rational self-examination and irrational vanity
in the light years between humility / mediation / compromise
and the arrogance and conceit that turns into violence
in the nanosecond between a sober second thought's moderation
and a knee-jerk of abuse
in the ironic, humorous coin flip between clever & stupid
in the journeys between confidence & arrogance, truth & deceit
in the shift of perception between music & noise
in the expanding cracks between virtue & self-righteousness
in the distance between free-swinging & unhinged
in the microscopic distance from a healthy cell   to cancer
in the infinite consequences of the cleaving split of an atom   a big bang
in the space between worlds, planets, solar systems
between your ego & my empathy   your reasons & my emotion
my logic & your entitlement to your feelings
between understanding & misconception
in the relativity between millennia & the blink of an eye
between what is stillborn & what remains beyond imagination
between the praiseworthy & the rueful

mind the gap

there live the ghosts of chances: the dreams of a future
what might come to be and what remains beyond imagination

mind the gap

there live the possibilities of the imagination
a whisper that promises a symphony
the infinite potential of the creative, biological, evolutionary imperatives

in the seam of a concrete sidewalk
there's a windblown seed, waiting on a drop of rain
a tiny ray of sunlight

The Good Fight

Because tomorrow the sun will rise.
Who knows what the tide will bring?
—CHUCK NOLAND, IN THE MOVIE *CAST AWAY*:
SCRIPT BY WILLIAM BROYLES JR.

the good fight is ours to choose
energy channelled into the social contract
to do no harm
to weigh the golden rule
to reinvent the perimeter
when the security of the castle wall
is being compromised

choose the face of your god
beyond one of religious dogma
or corporate business survival
beyond the frontiers of space and time
one incorporating the abyss, the black holes
the infinite challenge
of finding, and fulfilling
a puny presence on the timeline

the good fight often comes down to the simplest of choices

to keep breathing
to just get up on one's own two feet
        and put one foot
                out ahead of the other:
                                to move
                                        forward

Willing

they say "if god is willing"
but what they mean is if their *imagination* is willing
for any understanding of god is surely, simply
a product, a figment, of their imagination

or maybe they mean
if the random chaos of the universe is willing
if *fate* will allow
because *fate* is as haphazard as dumb luck
a bounce, good or bad
a card from the dealer's hack
a roll of the dice
a butterfly effect

serendipity doo dah

in this neck of the woods (last i checked)
their odds of getting terminal cancer are one in four
their odds of committing suicide are roughly one in 9,724
their odds of getting hit by lightning are one in 313,250

their god—their imagination
the arbitrary happenstance of their universe
their fate and their luck
are *all* willing
to allow those odds above
to get nudged by *their* determination

their will
          until
                    beyond their last will and testament
beyond their own determination
                                        their own will
                                                  will no longer
                                                            be willing

God's Will

with respect to the metaphysical
the supernatural
the transcendental

whose god is willing
cancer, hurricanes, earthquakes and tsunamis
and stupid human tricks
like warmongering?

whose god is willing
the ignorance of fundamentalism?
the zealotry of *any* - isms?

whose apocalyptic god is willing
conquest, famine and death
disease, plague and pestilence?

no god

god? no

Whose God?

Canada is legally, systematically, federally founded upon the imposition of supernatural power:
"... principles that recognize the supremacy of God ..."
—PREAMBLE TO THE CANADIAN CHARTER OF RIGHTS AND FREEDOMS

yet the will of god
that lofty notion of supremacy
is only ever
in the fallible corruptible hearts & minds of human beings

so ... whose god reigns *supreme*?
the one who requires very specific fasting, or
the one who comes in the bread & wine of the
sacramental host?
the one who requires male or female circumcision?
the one who requires the hijab, niqab, burka, al-amira,
shayla, khimar or chador?
the one with no shaving? or the one with dreadlocks?
a payot? or tonsure?
the one who allows bacon with eggs?
the one whose minions flip-flopped on witch-burning
and fish on Friday?

none of the foregoing irony of this historical context
can shake the determination of the faithful
for their god is all of these gods
and yet—*supremely*—none of them

is there a god for ants in their colonies
termites in their mounds?
how about a god for workers
in their towers of Babel, Shanghai and Canton
their cathedrals, castles and crystal palaces
their space needles,
their Burj Khalifa, their Abraj Al Bait, their trade centres?

The sun was a god
until it became common knowledge that Old Sol was simply a G2V star
mostly hydrogen & helium, burning as a fiery, molten, life-giving
gravitational-solar-system nuclear reactor
that had been around for maybe 4.6 billion years
with maybe another 5 billion to go
till this solar system becomes old news
to human beings and all of their gods
(and ants & termites & all the rest of Old Sol's living creatures)

of course—all this science means nothing
to so many true believers of their very own god
there is, still, a flat Earth society
and those who believe dinosaurs and holocausts are hoaxes

the Bible / Koran / Talmud is the literal word of god
interpreted by the faithful
and if you don't accept that
they might have to kill you
despite what it literally says in those books—
and none of *that* irony means literally anything to them either

because—y'know
those god-fearing folks over there are insulted
if you lump 'em in with the god-fearing folks over *yonder*:
because even though we're all one, under the supremacy of god
we still need the sects & denominations & brands & team logos
the churches, temples, cathedrals & real estate
in order to differentiate & define principles of supremacy

anyway—whose god
in omnipotent omniscience, perfect will and everlasting goodness
specifically requires *my* worship & praise and *my* unquestioning loyalty?
because—while apparently, there is no god but yours—
i can't help but wonder

which god might offer me freedom from gods?
because—maybe there *is* no god
except—maybe—the money & the real estate
to build the power to impose the one god
to rule them all

Beyond Reason

you can't reason with some human nature
that refuses to acknowledge the nature of things
because of their beliefs
in the supernatural

you can't expect common sense from acid tossers
racists, misogynists
abortion clinic bombers
jihad assassins of Charlie Hebdo cartoonists

you can't negotiate with terrorists

you can't reason with gun lovers
or the corporate officers of big pharma
who have become unnatural & cold-blooded
because the fiduciary duty of board members
(to return a profit to shareholders)
is a higher calling

similarly, you can't reason with the religious
because

they fail to recognize the fundamental common denominators
that link them to the non-negotiables (*the basket of deplorables*)
but they all have their higher-calling reasons
and their reasoning is a source of pride

so they will never see
just how unreasonable
they *all* are

Pendulum

The fundamental cause of the trouble is that in the modern world the stupid are cocksure while the intelligent are full of doubt.
—BERTRAND RUSSELL

we've lost that internal resting place of calm, balance
our clockwork gears have been ground so far down
that the arc of our pendulum swings wildly, uneven
goes too far
gets stuck, then worse
accelerates at the speed of light
out of control
from one extreme to another, it flies
from our compassion for humanity
philanthropy, forgiveness, optimism
brotherhood

to

misanthropy
pessimism
negative anger towards
stupidity & willful ignorance
& selfish greed & plain evil

time itself has lost its meaning
its metrics are unreliable
its rhythm can't be counted upon
it's impossible to find balance
on a planet in crisis
where fundamentalists wage war on
liberal democracy
and capitalism can't resist its fundamental urge
to kill and eat its young

Think of how stupid the average person is,
and realize half of them are stupider than that.
—GEORGE CARLIN

The Skunks

it's not a fair fight
the skunks come shuffling and snuffling
in the dark of night
and destroy the lawn
tearing up the sod
digging for grubs

be careful
our neighbourhood is rife
with their kind

the dog surprised one
behind the shed
a while back
and the stink lingered
for weeks

there are not enough successful predators
of the grubby skunks
they forage at will
and we are at the mercy of their nature
and poor eyesight
you've got to give them a wide berth
respect their terrible power
their ability
to ruin your habitat
with their stench

be careful

our culture is rife
with their kind

The Accident of Birth Is No Accident

genitalia begets defaults
into broad-brush categories of suspicion:
careful—could be one of those
cruel, insensitive, unenlightened ones

also looks like that genitalia could be
descended from peasant-class farm labourers
maybe old white-trash colonial settlers
inappropriately appropriating the storyline

oh, go on then
take generations of culpability
and whistle into the prevailing wind
bay from the doghouse
dog-paddle up shit creek
and drift on a Mark Twain raft
with discounted words

narratives will get rewritten regardless
types will be cast & recast
since the guilt of birth
is no accident

original sin
lives and breathes

now *there's* a bone to pick

PART 4

Inside Out
Exercising, Exorcising

lower case i

welcome me back
(how can i get more of *me* in here?)

i
i indulge in it
exercise it
exorcise it

i write what i know
i know my own mind
don't i?
i make it up (sometimes)

i might suggest
first person singular
limits the damage
keeps one humble

but—i of the beholder—
too much i makes me read
ego-man-i-acal

i y-i
y-i y-i ***y-i***

Identity Theft

Celebrity is a mask that eats into the face.
—JOHN UPDIKE

| who are you?   depends upon   which story's getting told   cuz some
| versions of you got stolen away—some others, you knowingly sold   *some folks*
| recognize your masks, your props, the marotte of a fool   still,
| others might see the didact   who took all that to school
some-| times, you gave yourself away   there's no mistaking that   but it's
| fair to say you could display the moves of an acrobat the
| instincts of a chameleon, or a *zelig* diplomat

con-| sider Jesus: carpenter? rabbi? son of god?   so then
it ap-|pears a question of *who*   might be more a question of *when*.
Yoda,| Ghandi, Chauncey Gardiner—first impressions can mislead
but | even a snake oil salesman is meeting a market need
the | eyes of beholders take   whatever they damn well please
| clothes can make the man yet offer the shallowest guarantees

the verse requires a chorus—the bridge leads to a lift
the nature of evolution   gives us a curious gift
to seek out the divine   unpack the infinite jest
and *so* on   and *so* forth,   never *ending* without rest
to peel away the onion till the onion is no more
just skin that's torn & shredded   lying scattered on the floor

well—yes, the   sums are greater than the parts
which is   somewhat problematical
that's   why it's metaphysical
and   not just mathematical

so | some might ask: who were you?   in your stolen moments of time
in your | stories of Whitman's multitudes   and poems that struggled to rhyme
you | only know that you have to go on the record as nature leads
pro- | vide a moving target as the grand parade proceeds
for | time will steal away whatever made you who you are
and | holding on to yesterday   won't get you very far
de- | fine yourself in the hearts & minds of the people that you love
that | oxygen travels through the mask
and | down *into the blood*

Who We Are (Seven Circles)

more than what we do
what we think
what we feel

we are also what we don't do
out of fear & doubt

each of us, atomic units
planets of hydrogen, oxygen & carbon
where seven orbits
intersect, circling & cycling through

we are the children we were—
the adolescents, yearning & learning
the mistakes that marked us
the damage inflicted

we are these bodies

wearing down, wearing out
we are the victories won
& the scars collected—earned
we are—each of us—
a location where fate & random chance collide

we are what we have known
the goodness
& sweetness tasted
the bitterness & sorrow
endured—survived

we imagine that we have
the infinite within us
even as life humbles us
within our realization
that imagination
                    is definitely
                              finite

Blood Whispers

to the children of my children's children
i bequeath some past indicatives,
present imperatives and interrogatives:
future conditionals and prevailing subjunctives.

the ghosts of my ancestors
haunt the nucleotides in the rungs of my DNA ladder.
my progenitors worried over gods and devils,
imagining them as external forces:
eternal entities battling in dimensions beyond human comprehension—
when, in reality—in truth—
stories of good and evil got cooked up in oh-so-human veins
conspiracies hatched in the very marrow of their bones.
rivalries of our spirited debate
have always been products of our own ingenuity,
a veritable vortex of greedy vice and contested virtue.

at this juncture, i struggle to climb the ladder
—imagine the unimaginable—
in relative illusions of time, with words and music
conjured between an ineffable past
that stretches back: maybe to a big bang
—maybe an infinite cycle of big bangs—
then forwards, along an infinite line,
picking up steam at the speed of light
running towards unborn generations
in the unknown.

if i may be so bold, let me take this window of opportunity
to leave my calling card . . .

i'm here. this is what my here looked like,
felt like, smelled and tasted like.
i hope you can hear me okay.
i hope you can read me right.
this is where i laughed
and cried and grieved and danced and scribbled out
the notes playing in my head
and the words that awaited the stroke of pen or keyboard
or guitar string.

i wish to address the time when you will be there
and i will be gone, with only my words and music left.

manifestos may well be collecting dust there, but
my ghost will be in the nucleotides
that form the rungs of your genetic ladder.
you might hear the whispers in your blood
feel the debates raging in your imagination.

i have no expectations: i can only hope
that these strokes and scribbles here
might weigh enough to tip the scales
convince you to choose the virtuous
the ethical—the moral—
the integrity of humility
running towards unborn generations
in the future unknown.

(i now return you to the regularly scheduled programming
of digital assault in your every waking moment.)

Blind Faith

he used to get in his twentieth-century car
turn the key and go
with no real knowledge of the mechanics
of the combustion engine
just acting in good faith

now there's a twenty-first-century button to push
and even less awareness of
the technology inside the digital electronics
driving the computer, powering the machinery

just click the mouse: tap the screen
then descend and venture through layers of code
gaining blind ignorance, losing confidence

he can only think in metaphor
within a metaphor within the code—
the jargon, the arcane, turf-protective
boilerplate bafflegab

there are no signposts
the road maps don't show where there be dragons
the new gods are disguised—encrypted
Mercury in league with Nike
guiding souls to the underworld

the deeper the dive—the faster / higher / stronger the mighty spin
of the new gods' powerful greed—
the more his trust becomes lost

he begrudges the relentless assumptions and impositions
stiffens in resistance
grows less & less inclined
more unwilling to suspend his disbelief
the only thing he knows for sure
is the immensity of his ignorance

there's no more good faith
                              now it's all   only blind

The Transient Moment

Puerile diary entries
Imagine the banal as profound
        so be it
a Catskills comedian might frame this one as
a true story that really happened to me
~ ~ ~ ~ ~ ~ ~ ~ ~ ~ ~ ~ ~ ~
maybe a quarter mile away, in my sightline
one leaf on a tree—one amongst the multitudes
beckoned in the breeze, catching the sun
like a hand, waving, fluttering, insisting
come here: *come here*

that day, there, right then
it was full of life
full of the transient and ever-changing flow
of the eternal essence of the universe

just one leaf, amongst the countless infinite foliage
just one leaf, a half a mile away
catching the sun *just so*
just in that moment—trembling, inviting

and then the wind changed
the clouds shifted the angle of the light
and the moment between us passed into the forever

but just for that moment
i was that leaf
                and the leaf
                        was me

just for this poem
                i was that moment
                                and the leaf was you

Mom

a kid going into grade one
didn't want mommy to leave the new classroom
hid in her skirt   was afraid of the world

she took him to choir practices at the church
talked him into being in the Sunday school Christmas pageant
taught him how to sing harmonies in "Bendameer's Stream"
as they washed & dried dishes after dinner

the second of three sons—the one with her artistry in him—
the one with her empathy and sensitivity spilling out
between the ages of three to eleven
(before his adolescence started boxing it back down)
was the child she wanted—a friend she needed
desperate to be her golden boy
because her first-born was a heartbreaker

that high school kid had the prettiest mom
in all her modesty and humility, she knew
she still had some of her 1940s cheerleader looks
even the old guys in church and the men in the stores
gave admiring second glances

but then the golden boy became a jock—then a musician
and in selfish rebellion, betrayed her   and her values

in his late teens, still living in the parents' home
coming in late from band rehearsals or gigs
she'd be sitting up in bed reading, writing in her diary
her husband dead asleep, sometimes snoring
she waited up—a worrier: chronic insomniac, catastrophizing

but after sharing a bit of whispered talk, pals again—conspirators

she could never quite understand the man he had become
but she was forgiving
he could never find a way to relieve her fretting anxieties and sorrow
so he just adopted them and remains his mother's son
looking for ways to forgive himself

His Mother's Diaries (the damage to & from)

one spring—after his father had been struggling
as a lonely, helpless widower for a few years
the basement in the old bungalow flooded
and a few lifetimes of keepsakes in cardboard boxes got waterlogged

the old man could not bring himself to assess the damage
one box in particular contained his wife's diaries
so—awkwardly, he asked his sole surviving son to go through them
to see what might be salvaged

a son should never agree to cross invisible lines
to see his mother in the beauty of her own lovely, loopy cursive script writing
as a young girl, becoming a woman
so naked, so unworldly, so ordinary in thought, word and deed

worse—to see himself as a teenaged villain, a monster
breaking her heart in his own quest for freedoms
a routine chapter of life that she and her husband could never fathom
the generation gap written into the watermarked (tear-stained) pages
if the words were never meant for his eyes
why did she bother to write, box and save them?
why did circumstance assign him to damage control assessment?
what is there to learn from such an education?
that he possesses the same compulsion for exorcism?
a poet's truth? damage shared along the way?
process, assess, attempt to control the trauma—publish or perish

conflicted, he threw out all the diaries, which seemed
a painful but dutiful kindness, as necessary as interment

what was private and secret in life became testamentary autobiography
forcing him to reassess from without and within
furnishing the lowdown on the damage that love eventually inflicts
the intimate knowledge of his late mother
her perspectives on her aging husband and her family
the disease that would eventually kill her
how could this unguarded unmasking end up as banal as recycled paper waste?

this education now shapes his thought, word and deed
was this her motivation and intention   all along?

Robert Edward Emmett

my older brother was always an enigma to the family
as a child, Robbie was a slow learner—struggled, and never caught up
just kept falling further behind
almost always passive, it was all moving too fast for him
didn't get most of it—couldn't catch it—couldn't help himself
his thousand-yard stare went through you
just a neutral, bypassing gaze, waiting on whatever might come next
        destined to be the family's black hole
        someone who would slip through the cracks
        and disappoint hopes, evade best intentions
                he wasn't bad—no evil bones in his body
        not entirely guileless—but not enough cunning to be devious
        his life became a recurring recycling story of self-inflicted loneliness
        usually lost somewhere, beyond the current reality
                he was a victim, waiting for the next accident of ill fate to come along
there are some people in this life that you cannot save from themselves
and that young man descended into a darkness that settled inside
never fully knowing what he was doing so he didn't know how or when to stop
in the family, everyone took a turn trying to be his saviour
but he was a full-time job that drained you of your own life force
eventually breaking your heart, crushing your spirit
and you had to cut him loose or he would destroy you too
inevitably, everyone came to the same realization
you had to let him go—hope he would bounce when he hit bottom
and learn how to help himself
he survived down there, somehow—never fully grasping his own fundamentals
never understanding, never mind controlling, the nature of his black hole
taking a few decades to realize
just how destructive it was on those who loved him

after completing all of the twelve steps (several times)
and still believing in a higher power
he apologized to everyone that his addiction had harmed
then—riddled with disease and ignoring his meds
finally saved himself from himself   and went to meet his god
now the nuclear family members are all gone
but the enigma of my brother lives on
in my survivor guilt

Ticket to Ride P.S. (In Favour of M.A.i.D.)

February 2021—my father died
faded out, pale and ghostly
moaning shifting & agitated   itchy, scratching
(they said those were common side effects of the drugs)
his body was riddled with maybe half a dozen conditions
something would finish him, take your pick
on the death certificate, the retirement centre's doctor chose *inanition*
(now there's a word you don't hear every day)
pop had gone full circle—reverted to a helpless baby once again
without the brain function for language
wore right out at ninety-two, long past a reasonable expiration date

for us, it was horrifying and inhumane torture
that he could not be spared the bleak, isolated, protracted misery of his decline
he wasn't dying alone, exactly: but in Covid epidemic circumstances
we could not provide the comfort his dignity deserved
his suffering became our grievous frustration

he gave me life, its glory and joy
the infinite gifts of a conscientious imagination

yet—also, of course, all of its heartache and sorrow

my loss came to rest in the centre of my chest
an ache settled into my bones
my soul went searching for something lost
in a valley of gravel & stones

the estate settled on sagging shoulders
to execute as seen fit
i'll play for time: learn how to accept its agenda
as i work out a balance to lighten the burden
of the one-way ticket to ride

In My Father's Voice

I loved the open fields of Etobicoke
where I raised chickens with my big black dog, Foam.
the life I learned to live in childhood and adolescence
anchored in duty, responsibility and loyalty.
I slowly chewed every single mouthful they put on my plate.
I carried my burdens of sadness without complaint or confrontation.
These were the virtues of Presbyterian stoicism
which governed all of my days.
When I played hockey, I was a goalkeeper,
and never went on the offensive.
I went along, to get along
on a charming smile and the lightness of my wit.
Thelma Margaret Baxter was the love of my life
and together we built a family of three boys
through the baby booming 1950s, when everything seemed possible.
I was devoted to the provision of necessities
through painstaking bookkeeping.
I always kept the careful privacy of my own counsel
indulging only in simple pleasures:
food and drink, the company of trusted friends,
holidays, a good game on tv, the daily paper,
and a strong cup of coffee.

I took comfort in the notion
of a living memorial
in the loving thoughts of those who knew me best.

I hope you might still hear my voice
turn a phrase you recognize
and you can lay the blame on my DNA
for that twinkle in your eyes.

The Inheritance

the inheritance includes
dad's cynicism and stoicism
his only-child loneliness and
repressed suppressed emotion
there was also mom's cheerleading optimism
her buoyant beaming smile

through both of their depression-era childhoods
and WW2 rationing
then during their teenaged innocence and naiveté

opposites attracted

and it's a good news / bad news thing
emerging from the best and worst of two solitudes

i get to be

conflicted

PART 5

Beyond Me

The Daily Grind

the daily grinding companionship
of the crunching crackle of crepitus
confirms
that the imagination is the only good playground left
but even that often degrades into hiss & static
with the signal fading in & out

meanwhile—what to make of this?
proceed with care
along different paths with different priorities, concerns—
a lowered voice, an unsteady gait

journeys are more instinctive, less ambitious
begun in vagaries, obscurities, allusions
intuiting destinations and making discoveries along the way
resolved to offer less words (less punctuation)
less opinion, more thought

yet, the endurance of spiritual asceticism
gets compromised
as the human body cannot withstand
the judgments of idealism
based on the science fiction
of *time travel*

but let's try not to dwell
                                        on the painfully obvious

Early Onset

the lighting in the warehouse doesn't reach into some corners anymore
lost amongst the stacks
pondering the forgotten
unable to locate uncertain nouns
persons, places, things
which aisle? which shelf?

unable to form decent enough parameters for a google search

what happens when the walls have dissolved
between what's real and what's a dream?
don't even recognize the warehouse
no familiar landmarks
only a vague terror
in the declining awareness
that it's all slipping away
fading into oblivion

staring at this poem
                    not even knowing
                                        what the words
                                                            mean

Meaning

so what do the words mean?

meaning is in motion
meaning arises within you
eye of the beholder
ear of the listener
subject to the interpretation of the
party of the second part

what i meant
originally
was a rock
in a sunlit garden

but the rock turned out to be a diamond
and the garden turned out to be Gethsemane
and the warm glow of a bright summer day
could be morning or, just as easily
the golden honey of a late afternoon
and that's what meaning is
that's what meaning does
meaning is
a moving target

On Needs & Wants

humanity
on this planet
needs more virtue
more humility
more good faith behaviour
more compassion

but we will never get
what we need

because too many of us
keep taking
what we want

Currency

quand j'espère que je peux devenir	when i hope i can become
quelqu'un que je ne suis pas	someone i'm not
je dois essayer	i need to try
de ralentir les choses	to slow things down
dans les espaces entre	in the spaces between
la vraie nature des choses	the true nature of things
l'espace entre	the space between
mon rocher ici	my rock here
sur le côté de la rivière	on the side of the river
et le courant	and the current
qui se précipite	rushing by
ralentit les choses	slow things down
et puis peut-être que	and then maybe
je peux trouver	i can find
ce que j'ai manqué	what i have been missing

Flow

flow is a coping strategy
that generates positive feelings of productivity
enabling personal expression
when life seems restrictive, discouraging
or indifferent
flow supports attempts
to make sense of what seems senseless
confusing, depressing, stupid, cruel or evil
flow reinforces
a journey of discovery and intuition
towards insight and self-realization
flow enhances the courage of convictions
with an intelligence that doesn't normally occur
at regular speed in daily life
it slows process down, or
speeds it up, because it
steps out of the current of the atomic clock
flow channels the maelstrom
broken up or down
into digestible bits of meditation
like praying in words on a page
seeking metaphors inside metaphors inside metaphors
so that a little house of cards starts standing up
leaning against itself
flow builds connections
surrender to its currency
its transportation towards transcendence
and its elevation
to the metaphysical

Paris 3 AM—April 26, 2025

i'm having trouble falling asleep.
the streets of Montparnasse have come to rest
but continue to breathe
in the cascading halos of streetlamps
urban whispers
through the grates
like the slits, filaments and spiracles
of a great white shark

history informs the process of time passing
the night transpiring
conspiring

the evidence of the past is in the present
and you get the sense of what it carries
the future humming
in the wee small hours

what's your plan? what's your strategy?
what's the schedule for your agenda?
the evidence of time and energy investment
surrounds Saint-Germain-des-Prés
the qualities and values of delayed gratification
the persistence and dedication to work ethic

the evidence is overwhelming

the days of Paris in springtime
are packed with sightseers, tourists
suckers and remoras
i am but one in the schools
buffeted around in the currents

Paris maintains its narrative on a timeline
flowing like the Seine around Notre Dame
so comfortable with the resurrection of the past
but never, never asleep

no wonder the tour guide said—
this is what we love to do!
we all sit in cafés,
sip coffee,
smoke cigarettes,
and judge people!

It

it is
as if
we go
on or
in or
up to
an

old sad end
can you see
why our act was bad?
let the big war die
get out
and run
far off
one day, our aim
can map out and set
the new era

it's

on us

so

ok?

Surfing in Limbo (Leaning Into It)

my shadowland of dreams is grey on grey
the colour is all drained out
in the pre-dawn or the nautical twilight
like old faded black & white photographs

it feels like something strange
is about to start happening
it could be sinister, evil
horrifying

there are no details—just vague impressions
in a grizzled wash of anxious suspension

but give it fifteen minutes
and maybe the dawn graduates into the world

or maybe it's going the other way
and nightfall starts wrapping everything
in the comfort of black velvet
under the starry haloed glow of street lamps

it's the in-between—the grip of limbo—that's unsettling

i need to learn how to keep leaning into it
to keep feeling for the momentum
of the earth against the sky
the impassive, unrelenting sweeping of the second hand

i need to relax into the current of the light
go with the ebb and flow of the tide
with the changing
of the guard

Survivor Tree

a callery pear tree stands
in the plaza of the World Trade Center
a survivor of 9/11
it blossoms in spring
symbolizing hope
it speaks to the spirit of life

it says that gods of vengeance
malevolence and murder
will never vanquish good faith
for gods of poison are more false
than Dionysus or Aphrodite
Eros or Gelos or even Comus

the tree is leaning into it
the tree stands against blind fundamentalism
blasphemies of sanctimony

a solitary pear tree
bears its eloquent, natural witness
it says
cut down 2996 lives
and hundreds of millions
will rise in their place

a survivor tree speaks
          and it says
                    i am no infidel
                              the nature of life
                                        will win

The Magic of 3

act 1 the introduction

once upon a time
there's he & she & what comes to be between them
there's the time & place & circumstances
there's an eternal triangulation of this & that & also those
all the *who when where* gets set in motion, to deliver
what with a seedling hint or two towards *wherefore & why*

act 2 the body

then this happens & that occurs & oh, one other thing transpires
there's a growing architecture of the *rhythm, melody & harmony*
what & wherefore & why become even more perplexing
'*how*' gets complicated & unbalanced
tension grows as the plot thickens
[curtain: intermission]

act 3 the conclusion

so then the lights come up, blazing and action rises, climaxes
and the story resolves itself, one way & another
the narrative arc comes back down to a place of rest:
and if they do not necessarily live happily ever after
(entirely possible, at this point, but not mandatory by any means:
also, increasingly likely
that hints are dropped for a sequel, or even a franchise)
even so, as these stanza breaks clearly illustrate
the formula of 3 retains its magic
triangulating, to corral the narrative
surround the idea
providing a satisfying balancing
of the unbalanced

The Music Is the Wind, Bob

(One day, I got to interview the world-famous record producer Bob Ezrin)

Bob had said, *the artist is like a kite*
and the producer is holding the string
and i thought i was lobbing up a nice fat batting-practice four-seamer
that he could knock out of the park
so i asked him,
what's the wind?
he frowned and replied
you're stretching the metaphor too thin
so i said, oh—okay
and i let it go

but it seemed simple enough to me, because
another Bob had said, *the answer is blowin' in the wind*

so i was thinking
as i have always thought
music is the answer

i was thinking
the *music* is the wind, Bob
the music is the wind

i'd imagined that's what he'd meant, all along
guess not

Her Palette

she set off down a yellow brick road
under fluorescent Day-Glo rainbows
in a plastic technicolor toddler-toys world
        then in her goth teens
        when she started seeing red
        it was all black on black
        on black
as she grew into her power
she adopted the cosmopolitan chic
of monochromatic shadings, silky pastels
a chameleon of cool soothing greens
covering her detachment
seeking subtle distractions
accessories, to set off her eyes, her hair

it could have been a mid-life crisis, but for the longest time
everything she heard and felt came in shades of blue
mostly indigo, but also cobalt, sapphire, azure
royal Egyptian and Persian

        she settled, then, comfortably
        where the ocean met the sky
        and when her blue period receded she craved the palette of autumn
        gold, straw, brassy yellows
        pear, olive, maroon, burnt orange—russets
        all reds fading, decaying into brown
        tawny caramels, dusty merlots
        some chocolatey mochas or rich rosewoods
        accents to set off rich mahoganies
        her coffee with a touch of cream
        the tobacco sunburst of an old archtop guitar
        all wavelengths echoing into reverb
        grey on its way to white on the way to its fade to black

and she is content
that she has covered the spectrum
of her palette

Microcosms

(One of the dozens of things I learned from reading Lorna Crozier)

the detail of her imagination is so profound
it generates plausible alternate realities
dreamscapes
and in the space between conventional material reality
and the credible nature of her creativity
lies a supernatural ability to generate
        a very intentional   airgap

because there's also fertile ground
between what gets written down
                                        and what's left unsaid

and in the mighty power of humble words
those openings are far from empty
        that's where ideas live   where they breathe
            where the reader is invited in   and required to participate
                with their own voices   in their own head

these words remain an invitation
                                        to integrate imagination

                                            microcosms—
                                                    no small thing

Uphill Downhill

i find courage is actually the easy part
downhill
simple
because—often
there's no other choice
the choice has been made

or made for me

but it's also that—
once i realized
that gravity is relentless
i could just surrender to its nature

so—no
the harder part is the uphill battle
struggling against fear and doubt
pushing my Sisyphean boulder
of worry & stress, guilt & regret
handicapped by all that
cortisol in my bloodstream
plaque in my arteries
the quartz and feldspar
of granite in my heart

bravery gets easy
when i arrive at the top of the mountain
and choose to be like water
flowing
downhill

The Riverruns

the riverruns downhill
seeking its own level
taking the path of least resistance
assuming the shape of the container

like raindrops scuttling down a window pane
a tear spilling down a cheek
naturally compelled by gravity
obeying laws of motion
it gathers speed—picks up momentum
as if it can hear the whispering roar
of a Niagara coursing over a horseshoe gorge

there's constant circulation
surrounding and encompassing us
a purification and distillation
in the precipitation / condensation / evaporation / lubrication
baptizing and showering us clean in the rise and fall
over and over again

the hydrogen & oxygen cycles
the waves insist
the moon pushes & pulls
the ocean tides ebb and flow
in my very breath
the beatings of my heart
the heavenly body
the holy ghost
                    the riverruns

Grateful Acknowledgements

To my beautiful wife, Jeannette, for a half century of humouring, forbearance, accommodation and caring love as I continued to indulge my avocations.

To my wise and nurturing editor at ECW Press / MisFit, Michael Holmes—providing the platform from which I can dive into the deep end of my occupational pool. (He's always handy with flotation devices.)

To my copy editor, Emily Schultz—diplomatic and style-conscious while (literally) helping to keep me from making a fool of myself.

To ECW's Victoria Cozza for production direction, Jessica Albert for art layout, then after it goes out the door, Emily Ferko for sales and Claire Pokorchak for publicity.

It takes a village, and the chief who makes the village possible is publisher David Caron, to whom we are all much obliged.

Maybe it could go without mention, but, especially for this, my second published book of poetry, I want to go on the written record and express my gratitude for the poetry that inhabits nature and informs this extraordinary, infinite gift of life and our human imagination: the poetry that lives because so many others before me generated a history of creativity, of inventing new accomplishments and breaking old rules: the poetry in music and the arts: the poetry within the exercise of our senses and our intellect. I want to proclaim my delight (and my vexation and mystification) for the fact that poetry is out there, everywhere, waiting for me to find it, shape it, and give it expression: and while I readily admit that it remains elusive and ineffable—even then, I am so very grateful for the opportunities afforded to keep *Leaning Into It*.

This book is printed on FSC®-certified paper. It contains recycled materials, and other controlled sources, is processed chlorine free